T0413870

THROW A VALENTINE'S DAY PARTY

BY CHRISTINA LEAF

Express!

BELLWETHER MEDIA • MINNEAPOLIS, MN

Imagination comes alive in **Express!**
Transform the everyday into the fresh and
new, discover ways to stir up flavor and
excitement, and experiment with new ideas
and materials. Express! makerspace books:
where your next creative adventure begins!

This edition first published in 2023 by Bellwether Media, Inc.

No part of this publication may be reproduced in whole or in part without written permission of the publisher.
For information regarding permission, write to Bellwether Media, Inc., Attention: Permissions Department,
6012 Blue Circle Drive, Minnetonka, MN 55343.

Library of Congress Cataloging-in-Publication Data

Names: Leaf, Christina, author.
Title: Throw a Valentine's day party / by Christina Leaf.
Description: Minneapolis, MN : Bellwether Media, Inc. 2023. | Series: Express! Party time! | Includes
   bibliographical references and index. | Audience: Ages 7-13 | Audience: Grades 4-6 | Summary:
   "Information accompanies step-by-step instructions for various crafts and recipes for a Valentine's Day party.
   The text level and subject matter are intended or students in grades 3 through 8"-- Provided by publisher.
Identifiers: LCCN 2022048001 (print) | LCCN 2022048002 (ebook) | ISBN 9798886871852 (library binding) |
   ISBN 9798886873115 (ebook)
Subjects: LCSH: Valentine decorations--Juvenile literature. | Valentine's Day cooking--Juvenile literature. |
   Children's parties--Juvenile literature.
Classification: LCC TT900.V34 L43 2023 (print) | LCC TT900.V34 (ebook) |
   DDC 745.594/1618--dc23/eng/20221013
LC record available at https://lccn.loc.gov/2022048001
LC ebook record available at https://lccn.loc.gov/2022048002

Text copyright © 2023 by Bellwether Media, Inc. EXPRESS and associated logos are trademarks
and/or registered trademarks of Bellwether Media, Inc.

Editor: Elizabeth Neuenfeldt   Series Design: Jeffrey Kollock   Book Designer: Laura Sowers
Projects and Project Photography: Jessica Moon   Craft Instructions: Sarah Eason

Printed in the United States of America, North Mankato, MN.

TABLE OF CONTENTS

THROW A VALENTINE'S DAY PARTY!

Valentine's Day is celebrated on February 14 in countries around the world. For many, it is a celebration of love. People give cards and gifts. No one knows how the holiday started. Stories say that long ago, a Roman **emperor** would not let young men marry. But Saint Valentine married couples in secret. He became a **symbol** for love. The holiday honors him.

You can celebrate love for friends, family, and more with a Valentine's Day party! This book is filled with sweet activities, from candy-themed decorations to bright pink hot chocolate. You will find everything you need for hosting. Get ready to throw a Valentine's Day party!

TOP TIP

Look for this feature throughout the book. It will give you tips to help improve your projects.

MATERIALS AND TOOLS

To make your party projects, you will need some basic art supplies, such as colored cardstock and paper. You will also need some basic kitchen tools, including knives, spoons, cutting boards, and mixing and serving bowls.

You will also need:
- glue
- scissors
- pencils
- markers
- paints
- paintbrushes
- tape

CANDY HEART BUNTING

Extra materials needed:
colored cardstock
yarn
hole punch

Candy hearts are a **traditional** Valentine's Day sweet. At first, the candies were shell-shaped. They had paper messages tucked inside. Later, the messages were printed onto the candies. The candies got their heart shape in 1902. People still enjoy these message-sending candies around Valentine's Day each year. Make your own candy heart decorations with this craft!

1 Cut out six large hearts from your colored cardstock and write messages on each one.

2 Cut out three medium-sized hearts and three small hearts. Glue the small hearts onto the medium hearts.

glue

3

Use a hole punch to create holes in the top of each of your hearts.

4

Take three pieces of yarn. Thread three hearts onto each yarn piece. Loop the yarn through the hole, as shown, and tie a knot at the back to secure each heart.

FINAL

TOP TIP

Decorate your party room with your bunting. If you have extra yarn and cardstock, you can make even more to hang!

7

CANDY HOLDER

Extra materials needed:

1 plant pot
1 small glass jar and lid
hot glue
small wooden ball
candy pieces

Sweets are the most popular Valentine's Day gift! English **chocolatier** Richard Cadbury is said to have started this tradition in 1861. He painted heart-shaped boxes of chocolates to sell. People kept the beautiful boxes to store keepsakes. Today, heart-shaped boxes of chocolates are still popular. This fun activity helps you craft your own candy holder for your favorite Valentine's Day candy!

2

When the pot is dry, remove the jar lid. Then, glue the jar to the pot base, as shown.

1

Turn the pot upside down and paint it. Let it dry.

3

Paint the outside of the jar lid and the wooden ball. When they are dry, glue the ball to the lid.

glue

4

Fill your jar with candy, and then screw on the lid.

FINAL

TOP TIP

Fill your candy holder with candy hearts for extra Valentine's Day fun!

CUTE COOKIES

Extra materials needed:

For the cookies:
2 sticks butter (softened)
2/3 cups sugar
1 egg yolk
2 teaspoons vanilla extract
2 cups all-purpose flour
parchment paper
nonstick baking tray
heart-shaped cookie cutter

For the decoration:
1/2 cup pink melting chocolate
colored hearts or sprinkles

Today's sugar cookies were first made by German **settlers** in Nazareth, Pennsylvania, in the 1700s. They are now a favorite treat on many holidays! People often use cookie cutters to make them into fun and festive shapes. They may decorate the cookies with icing, sprinkles, or both. These heart-shaped cookies are a sweet addition to your party!

SAFETY TIP

Ask an adult to help you with this recipe!

1

In a large bowl, mix the butter and sugar until smooth.

2

Add the egg yolk and vanilla extract. Stir well.

3

Sift in the flour and stir until all the ingredients are combined.

4

Once everything is mixed, use your hands to press the mixture into a dough. Place in the fridge for about 20 minutes.

5

Preheat the oven to 355 degrees Fahrenheit (180 degrees Celsius). Roll the dough onto a clean surface, then use a heart-shaped cutter to make your cookie shapes.

TURN THE PAGE! ▶

6

Place your heart shapes onto a nonstick baking tray. You may need two trays for all of your cookies. Bake for about 10 to 12 minutes, until pale gold.

Once cooked, carefully transfer the cookies to a wire rack to cool.

8

Put the pink melting chocolate in a microwaveable bowl. Heat in the microwave for 10 seconds at a time, stirring regularly until fully melted.

9

Dip half of a cookie into the melted chocolate, then place on a sheet of parchment paper. Sprinkle with your chosen decorations and leave to set.

Repeat Step 9 with the remaining cookies. Once they are complete, place them on a plate for your guests to enjoy!

FINAL

TOP TIP

The cookies can be made ahead of your party. They will keep for one week in an airtight container.

HEART-SHAPED PIZZA

Hearts are the most common Valentine's Day symbol! Ancient Egyptians believed the heart held a person's love and memories. Greek and Roman **philosophers** thought it was the center of people's emotions. While science now tells us these beliefs are not true, many people still associate hearts with love. You can include this symbol in your party with tasty heart-shaped pizzas!

Extra materials needed:

For the dough:
4 cups of all-purpose flour
2 teaspoons dried yeast
2 teaspoons salt
1 1/2 tablespoons olive oil
1 cup warm milk
8 cups warm water
baking tray
rolling pin

For the topping:
pizza sauce
1/2 cup cheese, grated (mozzarella or pizza)
pack of pepperoni slices

SAFETY TIP

Ask an adult to help you with this recipe!

1

Mix the flour, yeast, salt, olive oil, and milk in a bowl. Slowly add the water, stirring with a spoon to combine the ingredients.

2

Once your dough is formed, place it on a floured surface and knead for about 5 minutes. Then put the dough back in the bowl, cover with a clean dish towel, and leave for 1 hour.

3

Once the dough has risen, split it into six balls. Flatten them with a rolling pin, then shape them into hearts.

4

Preheat the oven to 390 degrees Fahrenheit (200 degrees Celsius). Place your heart-shaped dough pieces onto a baking tray. Cover with pizza sauce and grated cheese.

5

Cut the pepperoni slices into heart shapes, then place them on the pizzas. Bake the pizzas in the oven for about 10 to 12 minutes, until golden brown.

FINAL

STRAWBERRY HOT CHOCOLATE

Extra materials needed:
1 cup strawberries
2 cups milk
1/2 cup white
  chocolate chips
sugar
red or pink food
  coloring (optional)
whipped cream
edible heart
  decorations
blender

People have enjoyed chocolate drinks for thousands of years! Scientists believe the first people to make drinking chocolate lived in what is now Ecuador. They found **cacao** in the Amazon **Rain Forest**. Later, the ancient Maya and Aztec peoples used hot chocolate in **ceremonies** and other celebrations. You can make hot chocolate for your own celebration with this sweet recipe!

1
Slice your strawberries and put them in a bowl. Sprinkle with sugar.

2
Put the strawberries in a blender, add a little water, and blend.

3
Put your milk and the white chocolate chips in a saucepan. Heat gently until the chocolate melts.

4

Once the chocolate has melted, add the strawberry mixture. Stir well.

5

For a stronger pink, add some red or pink food coloring. Mix well and then pour into your mug. Top with whipped cream and the edible hearts. Repeat Steps 1 through 5 to make enough for all of your guests.

FINAL

With Love

FRIENDSHIP BRACELETS

Extra materials needed:

4 embroidery threads of different colors
masking tape
cardboard

Friendship is an important type of love! Several countries celebrate Friendship Day on February 14 along with or instead of Valentine's Day. In Finland, friends celebrate by sharing meals or enjoying fun activities like bowling or ice skating. Show your friends how important they are to you by giving them these friendship bracelets!

Cut your four pieces of thread to 72-inch (183-centimeter) lengths. Fold all the threads in half, then tie a knot in the folded end. Tape to cardboard to hold the knot in place. Arrange the unknotted threads so the color order is mirrored on each side.

TOP TIP

forward hitch

backward hitch

Forward knot:
forward hitch + forward hitch

Backward knot:
backward hitch + backward hitch

Make sure that the color order is mirrored on each side

2

Start with the outer left-hand thread. Tie a forward knot. A forward knot is two hitch knots as shown below and in the Top Tip opposite. Tie forward knots in the next two threads.

forward hitch

3

You have competed your first knots! Your left-hand thread will now be in the center.

this thread is now at the center

TURN THE PAGE! ▶

4

Take the outer right-hand thread. Tie backward knots on the next three threads to create a row of knots on the right side.

backward hitch

5

Your right-hand thread will now be in the center. Tie the two middle strings together to join the two sides.

tie the two center strings

6

Your first row is complete. Now repeat Steps 2 through 5 on the outer threads, making sure you keep your threads in color order throughout.

first row

7

Your second row is complete. Now repeat Steps 2 through 5 on the outer threads, making sure you keep your threads in color order throughout.

second row

8

Your third row is complete. Now repeat Steps 2 through 5 on the outer threads, making sure you keep your threads in color order throughout.

third row

9

Your fourth row is complete. You should now see that your pattern is starting to develop. Now repeat Steps 2 through 8 on the outer threads, making more rows until you have reached your desired length.

fourth row

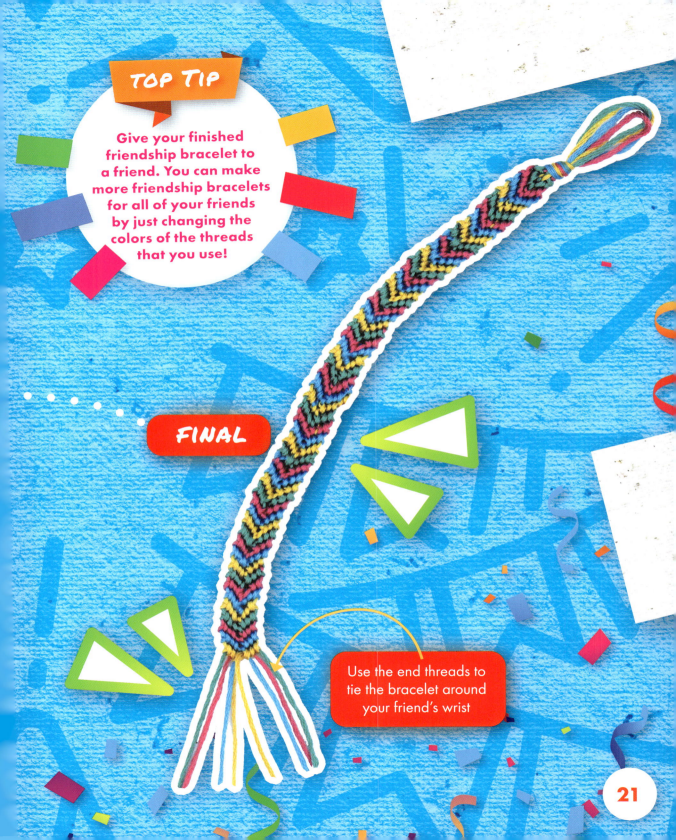

TOP TIP

Give your finished friendship bracelet to a friend. You can make more friendship bracelets for all of your friends by just changing the colors of the threads that you use!

FINAL

Use the end threads to tie the bracelet around your friend's wrist

GLOSSARY

cacao—fruit from the cacao tree; cacao is used to make chocolate.

ceremonies—acts performed in a regular way, especially related to social or religious events

chocolatier—a person who makes chocolates

emperor—a man who rules an empire; Ancient Rome was led by emperors.

philosophers—people who study ideas about knowledge, logic, and right and wrong

rain forest—a thick, green forest that receives a lot of rain

settlers—people who settle in a new place

symbol—something that stands for something else

traditional—related to customs, ideas, or beliefs handed down from one generation to the next

TO LEARN MORE

AT THE LIBRARY

Anderson, Shannon, MEd. *Celebrating Valentine's Day: History, Traditions, and Activities—A Holiday Book for Kids.* Emeryville, Calif.: Rockridge Press, 2021.

Borgert-Spaniol, Megan. *Super Simple Valentine's Day Activities: Fun and Easy Holiday Projects for Kids.* Minneapolis, Minn.: Abdo Publishing, 2018.

Brown, Tammy B. *The Valentine's Day Cookbook.* Mankato, Minn.: Black Rabbit Books, 2021.

ON THE WEB

FACTSURFER

Factsurfer.com gives you a safe, fun way to find more information.

1. Go to www.factsurfer.com.

2. Enter "Valentine's Day party" into the search box and click 🔍.

3. Select your book cover to see a list of related content.

INDEX

All photos in this book are provided through the courtesy of Calcium.